My Version
of Being a
BOSS LADY

IKHAQUANA STAR PRINCESS GLOVER

My Version
of Being a
BOSS LADY

ARPress
ILLUMINATING IDEAS
EMPOWERING VOICES

ARPress
45 Dan Road Suite 5
Canton, MA 02021

Hotline: 1(888) 821-0229
Fax: 1(508) 545-7580

Ordering Information:
Quantity sales. Special discounts are available on quantity purchases by corporations,associations, and others. For details, contact the publisher at the address above.

Printed in the United States of America.

ISBN-13:   Softcover   979-8-89330-168-7
            eBook   979-8-89330-169-4

Library of Congress Control Number: 2024900597

TABLE OF CONTENTS

Dedication iii

About the author v

Chapter 1 1

Chapter 2 5

Chapter 3 12

Chapter 4 14

    The tree of life… 20

Chapter 5 22

    The Night Life Scene..29

Chapter 6 30

    2005..31

    2006..33

    Back when 2007 34

    2008..36

Chapter 7 39

Chapter 8 41

    Memorial Weekend, May 42

Chapter 9 43

Chapter 10 45

    2015..47

Chapter 11 48

Chapter 12 49

DEDICATION

This book is dedicated to my first love Sapphire Star Williams-Glover. In November of 2013, it was a cold evening when the family and I went to have dinner. Myself, Sapphire's father, my mother, my two nieces, and my two nephews. The food at the restaurant was so delicious but it gave me heart burns. That night I couldn't sleep, I tried everything. My Lamaze instructor told me to listen to some soft music. I took a shower (nothing worked) By 1:30 am I was being taken to the hospital. That night by 7:56 pm my Star was born.

I also like to dedicate this book to my second true love Sky Princess Williams-Glover. Oh, she is so precious. She gave the most trouble when she was born. Doctors said, "Push" One hour later Are you ready to deliver this baby? *"Push"* Thinking to myself *"Push"* In July 2015 my second little girl was born… *"Sky Princess was her name."*

ABOUT THE AUTHOR

My name is Ikhaquana Star Princess Glover. Born to her parents in 1979. Jimmy Carter was the President. During that time women wore 2-4 inches, and the heels were sometimes even flat. Hotpants and bell-bottomed trousers were a popular fashion trend. Fashion back then was about individuality. Like today, there are no rules in the fashion game now. My mother and father had two children between them. I was the only girl. My dark brown hair, dark brown eyes and my light skin complexion is what I saw when I looked in the mirror. My make up is who I was....

CHAPTER 1

Princess is not only my nick name, but that is also my middle name that was given to me at birth.

"Why was I picked on?" I never could explain that even if I knew how to explain why girls in elementary school stared at me up and down. On the first day of school walking into my third-grade class, I had on a pair of black jeans, a nice shirt and new sneakers. I was trying to find my seat and a boy yelled out *"look at her Levi's"* everybody started laughing. I didn't have nothing to say. (It felt good because at least he thought they were Levi's jeans. My mother bought those on sale and those jeans wasn't even name brand.)

It was a little embarrassing but I just wanted to find any seat at the back of the class so I can tune him out. That day started as a bust for me but that school year I made a lot of friends. Not bad as I thought it would be. My mother found a two-bedroom apartment right across the street from the school's park. The elementary school I attended was located off the corner. In the middle of the block was a public park. Our living room window viewed the whole park. Everyday my brother and I asked to go across the street. We always got permission first.

Sometimes you had the hustlers, old timers and rough kids coming at different times day and night. My mother who was hard working wasn't always there to protect us from the danger in the streets. Especially at the park.

I had girlfriends who came to the park with their jump rope. We jumped Double Dutch and played tag. Hide-N-go seek was everyone's favorite. The school year was ten long months, but we looked forward to the summertime.

My mother got this new job, so my brother and I had to go to a babysitter's house. I didn't want to go to someone else house to sit down and do my homework. She was so kind. The lady offered us some soul food that was good to my soul. I loved her cooking and after a while of going to Ms. B house I felted at home.

Ms. B babysat for the whole neighborhood. She had two sets of foster children. Any time someone needed a place to stay, you can count on Ms. B's door open. Ms. B had seven children, four girls and three boys. One of her sons was so cute. (He reminded me of Bobby Brown. Dark skinned complexion, high top fade, big, plumed lips, always dressed in the latest designer clothes and high-top sneakers.) Although, I was young I started having feelings for nice looking guys. Into my teens we were still going to the babysitter. I graduated elementary and now going to junior high school, we were still going to Ms. B house after school. After all these years Ms. B children watched my brother and I grow up. Now her son who was so cute to me, name was Les. He had all the ladies. Some big, some little, some dark, some light and short. I always wondered, *"what does this man have that everybody wants?"* His style was unique. He matched every hat with his sneakers, his shirt was the same color as his pants. His lips were plumed. His eyes were gorgeous. His teeth were straight. I was only thirteen when I knew how I wanted him to notice me.

My boyfriend was tall, and he was a well-dressed guy himself. He always wore ACG boots even in the summertime. (Long jeans, nice t-shirts, no hats) He always had a nice clean cut. That was my first true love. He gave me something that I would never forget the day before my fourteen birthday. (It was called my first experience) I couldn't tell my mother, so I threw my dirty panties in the middle of the laundry basket.

It was a stain. I didn't know it was normal to bleed when you enter women hood. That relationship last for months until Trevor decided he wanted a family. I told him to go be with his baby mother. Yes, I said, "Baby mother" he had a newborn, and I didn't want to come in between that union. So, I told him thank you for our fun we were having but she needs you. (One time Trevor invited me to his house and in the living room behind the couch was a twin sized bed. I asked him, *who sleeps there?*" He said, *"A family friend"* He knew the whole time Keisha was living there and he couldn't tell me that he had a baby with her on the way.)

Now there was Sheriff. Player, Player, Playboy Sheriff. Light skin, cute face light eyes, curly hair. Well-dressed drug dealer. How did he lay eyes on me? One day after school, I was walking home from Junior high school. I was wearing a red jean skirt, nice plead shirt, stockings and black shoes. My hair was up in a ponytail. I was standing outside of my building, and he walked by. I was looking across the street and he asked me, *"how are you doing?"* my mouth was on the floor, I looked and could not speak. This guy started laughing and kept walking. I went in the house. I closed my room door and kneeled to pray at the edge of my bed. I said, *"Lord please you already know who I am. Do that again?"* Never ask God for something you are not ready for!

A few weeks went by, and I was coming from school. I see this guy getting out of a car and walking my direction.

He asked me *"could I walk you home?*

I asked him, *"who are you?"*

He said, *"I just want to be your friend."*

I said, *"ok, how old are you?"* He started laughing.

I asked *"could I laugh too? What is so funny?"*

He said, *"I think you are cute."*

The next day, I was walking through the hallway of I.S. 324 and every boy and girl was talking to me.

"Hey, how are you doing?" Girls smiling at me. Boys moving out the way to let me through. I was wondering where all the attention was coming from. Until the bully of the school yelled out *"that's my sister and nobody better not mess with her or else."* I looked at him.

I said, *"what?"*

He said, *"I know who you are."*

I looked at him with a surprising look on my face.

He said, *"my brother told me to look out for you."*

I asked him, *"Did Sheriff tell you I was his girlfriend?"*

He said, *"Yes, He told me you were his Princess."*

CHAPTER 2

Inever told Sheriff my middle name was Princess. But my mother always told me if it walks like a duck. Talk like a duck then it's a duck.

Being that my Riffy had his little brother Rahmel looking out for me. I had to walk like the Princess I really was. In the mornings before school, putting on extra Vaseline on my lips, extra gel on my edges and don't forget my name plate gold chain. Of course, my jewelry was on point. I had bamboo earrings, two rings on my left hand and two on my right hand. Arriving to school early was very important. I made first period before the bell rung. I was a math genius. I loved earth science but when it came to global studies I sucked. Current events and what's happening around the world really didn't seem important to me. Fourth period was lunch time. That was one of my favorite periods of the day. When we went outside for recess my Riffy came up to the school. I sometimes seen him passing something through the gate. Then he comes and walk my way.

"What's up baby girl?"

"Hey" I said, *"What are you doing up here at the school?"*

He said, *"You don't want me to come see my baby?"*

I said, *"I didn't know you were coming today, when I spoke to you yesterday you said you would not be around. I thought you were going out of town?"*

"Well, something else came up."

I said, *"Ok, how are you doing?"*

He said, *"what time are you coming to see me later? I'll show you how I've been feeling."*

I said, *"Ok I'll tell my mother that I have to go to the library."*

Now it was time for the next period. The bell rings, Sheriff watched me as I walked away from the schools' gate and entered through the door. We had gym class fifth period and I forgot to bring my sneakers. Gym was where I first learned how to play volleyball. (Trust me that's where a lot of girls took out their frustration.) If a girl didn't like you and you were on the other team. That time she gets the ball, she will make sure it lands in your face or hit you just because she doesn't like you. Although, I had a few associates, girls will try to cross you especially in gym.

We got to run, jump Double Dutch, sit on the sideline or exercise. Our coach wasn't strict but in order to pass the class- you had to participate in any sport. Some girls even played basketball. Just as you are having fun, Ring, Ring, Ring the bell rings. *"Everyone, enjoy the rest of the week and have a good weekend ladies."* said Mr. Triangle

Walking through the well-lit hallway, pass the lockers was the bathroom. I decided I needed to wet my face and hurry up to use the toilet quick. As I walked in the bathroom, I heard two girls talking about robbing the corner store. I went to the toilet stool to pee. I came out and Malanda was standing at the sink. Viola was standing by the door. I was washing my hands and Viola said, *"hit her."* I looked up and stared at Malanda.

She said, *"No not yet"*

Malanda, asked me *"how much of the conversation did you hear?"*

I said, *"what are you talking about?"*

Viola said, *"don't play stupid."*

I said, *"Who was talking to you?"*

She walked away from the door and into my face. *"Do you know who you are talking too?"*

I'm looking at her and said, *"why are you all up in my face with your breathe smelling like hot sausage?"*

She cuffed her hands and put it close to her nose to smell the hot air coming from her mouth. And Malanda walked around in a circle, then walked to the bathroom window with her back toward me and asked, *"Do you have $10.00?"*

I said, *"what? I'm late for class. If you would excuse me, please."* I continued to walk toward the door. I did not turn back, and I walked away. So glad that it wasn't a fight in the bathroom. If they wanted to jump me, they had the perfect opportunity.

My global studies teacher was in the middle of giving a test. The door opens and first thing he asked, "Where is your late pass?" I said, *"I just came from the bathroom and I'm sorry I don't have a late pass."* "Go have a seat and after class I want to talk to you." The test was hard because I didn't study. Only if I could see the girl next to me test paper but she was covering all her answers. I tried to do the best I can. I was filling in any answer so I could hurry up & finish.

Ring, Ring, Ring (so happy the bell rings)

Mr. Goldstein said, *"all pencils down"* *"I'll grade these tonight and hand all test papers back tomorrow. Be sure I get all test papers back by Friday."*

Later, that evening, I arrived home. Mommy was in the kitchen making dinner. I just wanted to be alone. I took off my clothes and laid down across the bed so I could fall into a deep sleep. I wanted to go out, but my body was saying something totally different. My girlfriend Mikco rung the downstairs bell. Ring, Ring *"Who is it?"* *"Me Mikco"* *"My daughter is sleeping."* I woke up to use the bathroom and my mother said answer the *buzzer. "Who is it?" "It's me Mikco, can you buzz me in? I need to talk to you."* My mother came back out the kitchen and asked, *"What's going on?"* I said, *"Mikco just needs to talk to me about something. Can I go out in the hallway?" "Yes."* My mother said. (She really didn't like us having company.) My brother and I had a couple of friends come over to the apartment. But my mother was the type of person not trusting too many people. She wanted to know who, what, when, where, and how? She gave everyone she met the third degree! Mikco came up four flights of stairs and there I was standing in the hallway.

"Hey girl" "What's up?" she said

"What are you doing over here?"

"Oh, I know you and Riffy are getting close."

"What are you talking about?"

"I see when he comes to the school on our lunch periods how he checks up on you."

I asked, *"How long are you going to be on this side?"*

"I'm waiting for my sister Nikky. She went to see her boyfriend, Ronald."

"Ok, do you want to walk with me to the store?" I asked

"Come on, go get dressed."

That's one thing I loved about Mikco, she was always ready. If it's about to go down all she needed to do was put her sneakers on. Mikco had a very smart mouth. She was one out of three sisters. She was light skinned complexion with sandy brown hair and hazel eyes. That girl knew she could get any shorty she wanted. Always wore the latest sneakers that came out. Her father worked for MTA and her mother was a nurse.

I went inside, I asked mommy *"could I go with Mikco to the corner store?"*

She said, *"Well it's a school night. Make sure you hurry up back. Oh, could you bring me some eggs?" "Here's two dollars and bring back my change."*

Walking down the stairs Mikco asked, *"Do you want to walk to the store on Gates Ave.?"*

"Well, what's wrong with the store on the corner?"

She said, *"There's a store on Gates Ave."*

I'm like "What if I see Riffy?" Girl, that's what it's about.

"Do you want to see him?"

I said, *"Ok"* So we walked to Gates Ave.

I said, *"I can't stay long because I have to buy some eggs before the store closes."*

We stood in front of his building as someone was coming up the block in the opposite direction. It was Sheriff brother Rahmel. Mikco said ask him.

I said, *"Is Sheriff home?"*

He said, *"I don't know where he is."* That's one thing about him that I couldn't understand. He was always on a mission. Sometimes home and other times out of town.

Mikco said *"stop being so shy."*

Rahmel asked, *"What did my aunt say?"*

I said, *"Your aunt? What did your aunt say about what?"*

Rahmel asked, *"Did you ring the bell?"*

I said, *"No"*

He said, *"Well how do you know he's not home?"*

I said, *"You are right, I don't know."*

Mikco phone rings. Caller asked, *"Are you ready?"*

She said, *"Yes, Nikky can you pick me up from Gates Ave.?"* I'm on my way.

We walked with Rahmel into the building and up the stairs to the second floor. He stuck his key in the door to the left. A lady was standing in the kitchen cooking. And Rahmel asked, *"Riff here?"* He was laying in the room knocked out.

Mikco phone rings. *"Where are you I'm outside."*

Mikco says *"I'm coming."*

I'm like, *"How are you going to bring me to Gates Ave. Now you are going to leave me? I didn't go to the store yet."*

Sheriff woke up and said, *"What's up shorty? I was getting up anyway. I'll walk you back home."*

I told Mikco I'll see her tomorrow. Anyway, I know I'm in trouble. Now it's 10pm I'm still not home.

"Well, I'm glad you finally came to see me." He looked and smelled good. He kissed me and then walked me toward the living room. He introduced me to his aunt. She said, *"How long have you known her? She's young and cute."* I smiled and Sheriff started laughing. He told her, *"I'll be back."*

He was a gentleman and walked me to the store. He bought the eggs and asked anything else? I said, "No thank you." He walked be back to my building and he kissed me again.

He asked, *"Am I going to see you tomorrow?"*

I said, *"Yes, I guess."*

He said, *"I like you already."*

"Oh, so you didn't like me before?"

He said, *"I like you better now that you came to see me."*

My mother was asleep. I took a long shower and went fast to bed. My nighttime prayer before I actually got in the bed was *"Lord, I thank you for heaven and earth and everything in between. Thank you for my mother, my brother, grandmother and for my enemies."*

CHAPTER 3

The next morning, I woke up around 7am to wash a handful of clothes. I didn't want to go to school because it felt like Friday was taking way too long to approach. I was walking toward the school building, my friend Althea said, "Good Morning" I responded, *"What's so good about it?"* she laughed as we both walked through the doors.

The bell to first period rings.

She said, *"You know we have a test?"* I said, *"On what?"*

"In Earth Science." Test, Test & more test. When is it going to stop? Well, you know we are only in the 7th grade. We have a few more years to go.

"Do you want to go to college after high school?"

"Well, yes."

"What do you want to be when you grow up?" Althea asked

"I want to be a lawyer."

"You know after high school, you have to go get your associates degree, then go back to get your law degree."

"Yes, Yes, Yes." I replied

As the day went on the Earth Science test was as easy as one, two, three. So glad that 8th period was over. I can go home to relax. Mommy stayed home today so we didn't have to go to Ms. B's. I wanted to go home so bad I did not want to make any stops along the way. I always got allowance, the only place I wanted to stop was a local corner store to buy some snacks. Mommy was making bar-b-que steak, white rice and broccoli. (I didn't seem to like steam broccoli as a kid.) My mother made me sit at the table and eat every bit. Whether the food got cold or not she always reminded us that there were people in the world starving.

My brother and I were sitting at the kitchen table one day. Mommy cut the television off and said to my brother & I *"This weekend I want to introduce yall to my friend."* My little brother asked, *"Who?"* She said, "Someone" We both said "ok"

She said, *"Well, we were talking for a little while now and I decided to bring my children into the picture."* I thought to myself, *"that's nice"*

Ring, Ring, Ring

My mother answered the phone. *"Oh, my goodness, Ok. Yes, that's no problem at all. Tell her to come, she can stay with us."* After my mother hung up the telephone. She said, *"I have to clean that back room for my aunt."* We were just looking at her about to walk out of the living room. Then mommy says, *"My aunt will come stay with us and I want yall to behave while she's here."* We said, *"what aunt?"*

"My mother's sister." She spoke

Rahmel called me one day and told me *"your Riffy went away for a long time."* I felt losted, only in the seventh grade and it seems like everyone is leaving me. Sheriff got locked up for selling cocaine to an undercover cop. He was put in cuffs on the corner of Stuyvesant and Greene Ave.

CHAPTER 4

When my aunt came to live with us, my mother had an in-house babysitter. Aunty B was great. She did everything, she cooked and cleaned. Laundry towels were folded and put in the linen closet where it belonged. My aunt made the best peach cobbler you could ever taste. She loved being in the kitchen. Anybody came over to visit, she would offer them food.

Mommy spent most of her time working. After work she attended night school. And that's when she met a boyfriend. Guy was in her speech class and that's where they hooked up. His name was Butch. He was tall, medium brown, one of five children. Real family-oriented type of guy. Lived on the top floor of his mother's two-family brick house. He invited us to his house to a bar-b-que. My mother dressed us up and arrived early. We sat out back and was introduced to the whole family.

There was a lot of food, we had hamburgers and hot dogs. They made sausages, corn on the cob, grilled chicken and ribs. We didn't like salads or vegetables at a cook-out. But we loved watermelon. (It was lots of fruits and icy's) The Ridley family made sure it was a kid friendly environment.

My brother and I were young, so we really didn't ask to many questions. Mommy continued her education in business and graduated with her associates degree. She provided for her family.

Made sure my brother and I went to our regular doctor appointments, went to school on time & had snack money.

Now as years are passing by, still living in Bedford Stuyvesant, Brooklyn. I'm getting older, doing well in school. Growing up and interested in boys.

Although, my aunt came to live with us, and we didn't have to go to Ms. B's house. I still went over to visit because her and her family became my family too. Besides, I loved her cooking. Her baby son became my crush. (I couldn't wait to go over to visit him because he would talk to me about all his bullshit. He would tell me that I am special.) I wore a brown dress on one visit to Ms. B's house and that day was very hot. When Les, saw me, he helped me take the dress off. He told me how nice I looked. And he wanted to show me how he felt. I couldn't tell nobody what he gave me because it was our little secret.

Pow, Pow, Pow

We was sitting in the living room watching television, my mother came out the back room. *"Get down, get down, nobody moves."*

My brother and I had to lay on the floor because my mother always said *"a bullet doesn't have a name on it. Bullets travel. So being that we lived on the fourth floor and across from a park. We didn't know where they were shooting from."* She said, *"I love this apartment, but I can't live over here no more it's getting too bad. Next summer, I'm sending yall down south."* My mother wanted us to experience the south where the pace is slower than the city.

Sometimes bums and crack heads use to hang out in our hallways in the apartment building that I lived in. No matter how many times the management changed the locks on the door downstairs they still yanked the door open. Ms. Virginia son on the second-floor use to go in and out. Ms. Pinky, on the third-floor son had a full-time job and he didn't bother nobody. Ms. D on the first floor always had company and on Friday nights she had her card games.

One day, my mother received a phone call from Ms. B. my mother was holding the phone saying *"Yeah, those gun shots was loud."* Ms. B. told my mother that Les left to go to the store and went to meet Keeta at the train station. He never came back.

"What?" my mother asked.

Ms. B, said *"They set my son up."* He received a phone call, and he was in his bed. He got dressed to go meet Keeta and someone said something. And that's when you heard Pow, Pow, Pow. Everyone, who was there started running and ducking behind cars and Les fell to the ground. No one could save him. He laid there until help came and no one heard from him again. I didn't know how to feel because I was too young to understand. I didn't have much feelings toward the situation. I enjoyed what he gave me, and I knew when he got killed I wasn't going to see him again. I wasn't going to touch or feel it again either.

In 1993, My mother knew I was a fan of Mary J. Blige and there were advertisements on the radio of an upcoming concert. Starring Mary J. Blige and special guest. My mom told me to ask Olivia (Ms. B's daughter) did she want to take me and of course she said yes. The morning of the concert I caught my monthly friend. I still wanted to go to the concert. I wore a nice shirt and jean shorts with all black reeboks. Olivia was wearing a Polo shirt and black shorts with a pair of orange classic reeboks. The concert was fabulous. Mary J. Blige, Biggie Smalls, En vogue and SWV performed at Madison Square Garden. What a concert? I would never forget. Thanks to my mother for buying us these amazing tickets and the seats was great.

Back then I use to get in trouble for listening to Shaba Ranks and Super Cat. My mother use to say turn that shit off. I loved music. My R & B at times and other times my Reggae. If there was a concert starring Jamaican artist my mom probably would decline. I promised myself, when I grow up, I'm going to take myself to a Jamaican concert if I hear about it.

My only rule as a teenager was *"whatever I say goes"*. If I wasn't feeling a guy, I would tell him my name was Tyesha. And I would give him a fake number. When I used to go downtown Brooklyn with my friends. I used to hear *"Hey Tyesha."* Looking around me like, *"who is that?"* I sometimes forgot my street name was Tyesha.

One day, I was somewhere with my best friend Layla and this guy approached me and said, *"I know your real name is not Tyesha. And that phone number you are giving out is the wrong number. Maybe you should change it."* I was looking at him like he had 4 faces. He said, *"that guy who lives there said that you must look good because so many guys call here for you."* (Layla looked at me like, *"Am I missing something here? Is there something you want to tell me?"*) After she started laughing, I said, *"thank you & have a nice day."* I didn't need him wasting no more of my time. I said, *"Layla lets go."*

We stopped in Burger King on Fulton Street to grab a bite. Then Layla with those 4-inch heels fell down the stairs. I said, *"Oh my goodness, Are you alright?"* (I couldn't help but to laugh.) She was not only embarrassed because of the cute guys in Burger King. But her curls in her hair was out of place. One thing about Layla, she always had a press-n-curl. My mother use to send me to the salon also, but I use to get a finger wave style or French roll. I was always a fly girl and so was Layla.

One cold day in December, Layla wanted to leave school early so she could go pond in her mother wedding ring. We went to Fulton Street in Manhattan. (That girl got paid.) I asked her, *"where are you going to tell your mom you got all that money from?"* She said, *"No need to explain, my dad sends me money."* I said, "Cool." I wished that I could put a couple of those 20's in my pocket. At least Layla offered to buy some lunch. It wasn't a problem for Layla, it came naturally. Coming to school with her ice burg outfits, hair was always on point but one thing. She was failing Global Studies. One day, I was up in the principal's office with my mother and here comes Layla with her mom.

First time me meeting Layla's mom was in the principal's office. I was also failing, but when we saw each other, we couldn't speak. *"Why?"* Because we both were there for the same reason. Her mother said, *"What's the distraction? Who is she? Who are you hanging out with? Do you hear me talking to you?"* Layla's mother wasn't no joke. She asked her so many questions and didn't give her no chance to answer not one question at all.

My mother and I weren't there that long. I know I was in trouble when I got home. I couldn't go outside; I couldn't watch no television, or I couldn't use no telephone. I had to do chores. My mother made me wash the dishes and clean the bathroom. I had to make my bed every morning. (It was a punishment and lesson at the same time. It was also called being responsible.)

When I was 16 years old going to Martin Van Buren High School. I skipped school one day and took myself to an S.T.D clinic because I wanted to make sure my citty cat was O.K.

I remember the night before I looked at three different places to choose from. The one place that I picked was off Hillside Ave in Queens. It was nice and clean. When my number was called, it was my turn to see a doctor. First question was, *"How many sex partners do you have?"*

I said *"One"*

Then I was asked, *"If you find out today that you have an S.T.D. would you harm yourself or anyone else?"*

I said, *"I'm going to kill him."*

Doctor said, *"Oh no. Honey you may need counseling."*

I said, *"Doctor what would you do?"*

"Well, I would just talk to him. But let me just ask the questions and you just answer them."

Next question *"If you need medicine for any reason, can we contact your parents?"*

I said, *"No."*

Doctor asked me for an emergency contact number. I gave the wrong number. I really didn't want my mother to know about this visit to the clinic. And if she knew I wasn't in school today, I probably would be in trouble. Doctor gave me a gown, told me to get undress and put these on.

I got undress and took out my feminine spray from my bag to spray my citty cat. I put the gown on and was ready for my first check-up!

Visit went well, Doctor informed me that there were no signs of any S.T. D's and cervix looks great.

"Young lady whatever you're doing, keep it up. Whatever you are not doing, don't do it. Be safe out there and here take some condoms."

I arrived before 10 A.M. and was out of there before 12 noon. Now time for lunch. I treated myself to BBQs in time square. (My favorite.)

THE TREE OF LIFE...

Back at my grandmother's house in Crown Heights, Brooklyn. (We called Brooklyn, Bk back in the days.) Every Sunday, For Sunday dinners, my grandmother used to burn the macaroni & cheese. (Everyone loved it.) Real cheesy but the thick layer on top was always dark. Fried chicken, collard greens and dried white rice was our traditional Sunday dinners. My grandmother enjoyed cooking for her family and anyone who came to visit. When she was in a good mood, we would have oxtails instead of fried chicken. Me and my cousin's loved to help make the cake because we got to stick our fingers in the bowl of the lemon mix. It was so good. Ms. Bernice's signature to a good meal was her chocolate cake. All the cousins, aunts, and uncles looked forward to moms favorite Kool-laid.

Ms. Bernice filled an empty milk container with two packs of orange mix and a lot of sugar. She couldn't stand when anyone came in the kitchen when she was in her zone. Mom kept yelling, *"What yall kids doing now? Sit yall asses still."* I could remember when she turned on the living room television then had all the children sitting on the floor to gather around. No sitting on the living room couch. *"No playing in the living room."* She would say. The first one to get up was going to get in trouble and no Kool-laid! Every Friday we had spaghetti. If we didn't like what was made, then we go to bed hungry. Although, my grandmother gave us a choice (this or that) If we didn't like it, we would go ask my grandfather. Charlie- pooh, use to ask us, *"What did mom say?"* She was the boss. Whatever she says goes!

The house was filled with cigarette smoke. Mom used to smoke Newport's and Charlie-pooh smoked Pall Mall cigarettes. The neighbor next door would knock on my grandmother's door. Ms. Mack would always borrow two eggs and sometimes a cup of sugar. One time she knocked on the door for a cup of milk. Seemed like her house was a soup kitchen. My grandmother had the heart of gold and did anything for anybody.

I could remember being ten years old when my mother first took me to the nail salon. She had the nail tech give me a manicure and pedicure. I got to choose the color but nothing too loud.

On Sunday mornings, I went to church with my grandfather along with my cousin. He used to give us five dollars for McDonald's. Every Sunday, we bought a happy meal. I loved Charlie Pooh, because he worked hard Sunday through Saturday. He was the man of the house, but my grandmother was the boss.

Monday through Saturday, Charlie Pooh, went to work in a local dry cleaner. And on Sundays, he had a position in the Methodist church downtown, Brooklyn. When my grandfather gave me a dollar – he always said, *"Save Fifty Cents."* He was teaching me how to save money.

During the holiday, everyone came to my grandmother's house. As a family before Christmas, we always did secret Santa. Whoever name you picked out the hat you had to give them a gift. We always sat around the tree on Christmas Eve wanting to open just one present…

CHAPTER 5

In 2001, there he was… light skin, corn braids (straight back) hazel eyes, tall and cute with a uniform on. Coming around asking for tickets, tickets, tickets. As I sat on the train headed toward Brooklyn, New York. He stood behind me *"Miss, your ticket?"* I said, *"Here, one way to Brooklyn."* This bother was not only cute, but he also had swag. He walked away and turned around, looked into my eyes and said, *"I'll be back."*

(Now anyone who knows me know I am shy, very wise, outgoing, down to earth, love good vibes, good conversations shopping, travelling, staying home and cuddling with the right somebody. Enjoying family and friends during the holidays.)

I'm sitting on the train, needing something to eat. Looking through my bag for a piece of gum. I came across a mint and here he comes again. *"Next stop is the last stop."*

As he made an announcement before he sat down right behind me. After five minutes, he asked me, *"Could I ask you a question?"*

I turned and said, *"What?"*

He said, *"Why are you so mean?"*

No comments.

He asked, *"is that your real hair?"*

I said, *"Excuse me"*

He said, *"I can't stand weave."*

I said, *"Wow, is that a part of your job to ask customers to whom you don't know about their hair?"*

He laughed.

He thought I was cute and funny. Not knowing it takes one to know one. (An expression I heard when I was growing up.)

He asked, *"Where are you going, and should you be in school?"*

We were walking in the same direction as we both exit the train. I told him that he asks a lot of questions. He was on a lunch break and offered to buy lunch.

"What is your name?"

"Oh, my name is Chris."

"Chris, what sign are you?"

"I am Virgo. What's your sign?" I asked.

"I'm also a Virgo, when is your birthday?"

"My birthday is in September." I said.

"Well, my birthday is also in September. What day?" he asked

I said, *"The 16th"*

He started laughing again. I said, *"What is so funny?"*

He said, *"That's my birthday."*

I said, *"Are you joking?"*

He said, *"Let me see your ID. I need proof of that."*

"We have the same birthday and that's your real hair."

I said, *"Lord, where did he come from?"*

One thing that I love about my heavenly father is when you ask him for something. He will give it to you. In secret, it is done. He may not come when you want him but he's always on time.

My aunt used to ask me, "Did I ask God for that?" I always stared at her.

I said, "God didn't answer." She always said, if it doesn't feel right then maybe you shouldn't do it. God does answer, all you need to do is listen!

We have the same birthday but just he is seven years older. As I looked in the mirror. I said, *"Ok he's working and girl you need someone with a job."* He called on the phone and said, *"Hey, are you ready for this ride?"*

I said, *"yes, I'm coming."*

I was in for a long ride. Not only did he have a royal blue LX. He came to pick me up on a red and black ninjas motorcycle. I had on a pair of old navy-blue denim shorts, white Guess t-shirt with a pair of white classic reeboks. I loved my reeboks. In high school, I had every color. The white with the purple at the bottom, the all-orange reeboks, the red ones and all black ones were my favorite. I had about three black ones at different period of times. I had an outfit to match every single one. When my mother use to give me my allowance. One week I bought a pair of jeans. Next time a skirt and then for my shoe game. I love shoes, my sandals for the summer was also crazy.

I had a shoe to match every dress. Having something to wear was never a problem. I had too many clothes in my closet. I can see every outfit. Every empty hanger, I had to buy something to put on these hangers. It was so sad as a teenager I was bossing up!

Chris was his name. I was ready for this ride, not knowing what to expect. The sound of the engine. Voom, Voom, Voom It got my insides throbbing. Ready to put my helmet on and hoop right on the back, we went riding to the park. Chris wanted to play a little basketball. As I sat on the bench and just watched him play.

After a half hour, Chris came running up to me. *"Are you hungry?"* I said, *"Sure!"*

He finished playing the game and was ready for another ride. Voom, Voom, Voom the bike started. As other people in the park were passing by, looking at me jump my fatty on the back of the bike.

We rode off down Springfield Blvd. He took me to his favorite place for some pizza. My favorite, I love a good slice of cheesy pizza. We talked, we had a slice, talked some more then we went riding again. The next stop was his friend's house. He wanted to show me off ofcourse. Next stop was his house.

Ruff, Ruff, Ruff, That Dog was huge. I stood outside the gate, and he put the dog around back where it belonged. He said, *"Come in."* I walked in the gate and then he pointed. I then walked up the stairs. As he opened the door and clicked on the light. The first thing that I saw was the living room (Beautiful) Nice furniture in the living room and I just wanted to use the bathroom.

He pointed and said over there. I used the bathroom and Chris came to the door and said, *"Do you need help?"* I'm like, *"No, I think I got it."* He said, *"You think?"*

I came out the bathroom and there was that look again, the same look he gave me on the train. He looked the same way at me when we went to his friend's house.

Chris was still in his living room and walking toward the stereo. He wanted to play some music, so he chooses slow jams. He played, *"Jaheim, put that woman first."* Then he gave me a tour of his house. Once, he introduced me to the bedroom. It was no need to elaborate on the rest. All I know is I woke up next to this man who worked hard, played ball and rode around for a few hours. I knew he was beyond tired. But I had no choice to wake him up because. I needed to leave. I knew I was going to get in trouble.

The next day, Chris called, asked me what was I doing? He came to pick me up in the royal blue LX. We went for some ice cream. He really enjoyed my company, and I enjoyed his.

Before you knew it, I was entering in his world, he was testing me to see if I was someone worth spending time with. The age of twenty wanting to open a salon was my goal. But I was only an hair assistant to a well-known minister Mr. D.

I was currently enrolled in hair school, working six days for Mr. D's salon and gained experience. I shampooed hair, blow dry, corn braid, pressed and curled hair all under Mr. D's license after school Monday to Friday making $150.00 in salary plus my tips.

Every day until seven o'clock in the evening was the last walk-in for any stylist customers. The shop located on Merrick Blvd. Walking distance from my mother's house.

But when you have a boyfriend driving you to work, there's never a time to walk or be late for any appointments. (I had the kids' section of the salon rocking with the latest music and creating my different designs.) I made so much money there I knew that I belonged. I always pictured myself running things. And that's when things changed. Mr. D started noticing me booking appointment right after another. He really didn't like that. One day, he stopped me from booking an appointment to go to the store to get him some milk for his cereal. I'm like, What? He asked me, *"What am I doing?"*

Mr. D. also had a list of other things he wanted from the store. I said, *"I'll go to the store after I'm finished with my customer."* He felt this was his shop. I felt that I was making my own money. He sat me down and said, *"If you want to work for yourself then pay for the chair here."* *"So put me on commission in your salon."* I said.

He didn't want that. So, one Saturday morning, I packed my things and left his salon with a couple of clients number in my pocket.

When I decided to leave Mr. D's salon. I thought six months was enough experience to be on my own, I went to another salon on Jamaica avenue. That lady was nasty., she was the owner of a very small salon with three styling chairs, a sink and two dryers. I went there with a few numbers I told the owner that I specialized in natural hair care. One day, a producer for a radio station walked-in to inquire about an all-natural hair style that would last her for three weeks to a month. Lady wanted the best person in the shop to do her hair. The owner pointed to the middle chair and then told me to drape her. I put a paper towel around her neck and a cape on to cover her clothes. The capes were clean because she just had Beatrice come back from the laundry.

The owner's name was Diamond, and she had an earring in her tongue. She was light skinned, real thick lady who wore a long black weave and flip flops. One thing about Diamond is she had a big nose and she was real nasty.

After I draped the lady, Ms. D said *"Now Beatrice, go take her to the sink. Wash and condition her hair."*

I wondered why Ms. D just didn't have the other stylist Beatrice didn't have drape her. Anyway, a small salon you can hear a pin dropped because that's how confined you are.

Diamond was always looking around her small shop to see what me and Beatrice was doing. After Ms. B finished blow drying the producer's hair. Diamond told her to sit back in the middle chair. I was reading a hair magazine. Diamond told me to give her a natural style. Not sure of what in particular she wanted to do to her hair. She then said, *"be creative young lady."*

I asked her, *"What is your name?"*

She said, *"My name is Tracey, Tracey Lewis."*

I said," *Ok, Tracey so you really want me to free style, right?"*

She said, *"Yes."*

After one hour, I reassured Tracey that I was almost finished, her eyes were closed, and she was just nodding. Enjoying getting her hair done like this was a first time in a long time. She was more than satisfied and paid for her style. She was walking toward the door before saying *"Princess can you come for a second?"* I got up from the styling chair and walked toward her at the door. She handed me a tip of five dollars and said, *"I'll see you next month."*

The Night Life Scene...

One night I got a phone call from my friend Jo-Jo and he asked me if I wanted to go to the city? I answered, *"Sure where in the city?"*

The first stop we drove to was 42nd street & 8th AVE. where people hung out to show off their new cars, SUVs, bikes and man showed off who had the hottest chick. I wore a Ecko skirt with matching shirt and my orange classic reeboks. I was there to make Jo-Jo look good. We weren't dating, he was just a good friend.

Jo-Jo was a nerd, he lived with his mother, he wore glasses, long sleeve shirts even in the summertime. He washed his mom clothes because he said, *"she needs help."* When I finally met Jo-Jo's mother she was a strong older lady. I just think when Jo-Jo grew up that mommy kept him doing house chores so he knows what to do when he gets married.

I loved hanging out with Jo-Jo, he always had money to burn. But, I never left my house without $25.00. My aunt always taught me to always take my friend penny with me when I go out. I asked, *"Who was penny?"* That's what she called emergency money.

The next stop was the China club, we didn't stay there long. But when the d.j. asked three females to come to the stage to battle in the dance competition for a prize. One girl, with her long braids went on stage and another girl was choosen and the d.j. looked through the crowd. He came up to me and said, *"This girl right here with the Ecko outfit."* I'm like, *"Wow."* Jo-Jo said "Go Princess." I went on stage and battled those two other girls and the music was playing "Fat Joe and Remy Martin" song "Lean Back." I won that competition. People in the front was throwing money on the stage. I stopped dancing to pick up my dollars. That night ended good and Jo-Jo drove me home.

CHAPTER 6

In 2004 May Memorial weekend Voom, Voom, Voom. Ready to ride, Now in Myrtle beach S.C. 9:00 A.M. We all had breakfast and all cellular phones were ringing. My phone rings. *"Are you ready?"*

I came downstairs out of my hotel. I called my friend, *"Do you want to go for a ride?'*

"With whom?"

"Dave and his friends," I said

"Girl, I'm coming."

Yes, that's what we did, we were riders. We rode on those ninjas, the speed was 110mph. Three O'clock in the afternoon bike BBQs at the racetrack. Tonight, at seven O'clock in the evening Hooters parking lot. The meet and greet was real. I told Neecy, Ria and Dee Dee what the plan was, and they went along with it. Dave had his crew, and I had my team also. Girls, women, men, riders, chicks' hoes and pimps. (Everybody was flooding their streets.)

At the racetrack I hopped off the bike the wrong way and standing so close to the engine. I burnt my leg. Yes, the engine of a motorcycle is a third-degree burn, I had on my pum-pum shorts and t-shirt with my sneakers. One thing about the south, it is always hot. 100 degrees you didn't want to wear no clothes. In the morning when I got dressed, I wore clothes for every occasion. We never knew where we would end-up

2005

Voom, Voom, Voom

There was a big bike blessing in Harlem, New York. One month before Memorial weekend. 1000 bikers are planning on attending this one. There were so many accidents in the last few weeks. Guys enjoy riding and doing stuns on the bikes. Showing off for these women. And when the weather is nice, Women wore no clothes. Showing off their bodies. Some showed off everything and leaving nothing to the imagination. I dressed simple, shorts and a t-shirt. (I was always ready to go for a good ride.)

One of my friends just had a baby in February. She planned to go with me to Myrtle Beach, S.C. for black bike week, but she didn't have a babysitter to watch her son. I had already paid for my bus ticket and hotel room. She was sure she would be able to go. Until one day, her mother found out she was going with me on vacation.

My friend and I use to dress alike. Ride with bikers all the time. But that all changed when she and her other friends went out one day. She met a pimp, and he offered her a place to stay, shopping, trips to the salon and a little pocket money. (I didn't know what was going on with her. I knew she met someone new who had money, but I didn't know to what degree. She was having so much fun with her new guy friend.)

One day we were walking to Popeyes her mother was driving and stopped her car on the side of us. *"Why are you still hanging out with this girl? What did I tell you about her? She is trouble."* Her mother rolled up her window and drove off. I looked at her and I said, *"What was that about?"*

She told me, *"Not to worry about my mom, maybe she is having a bad day."* I ignored it, but I knew something was behind it. I didn't understand, her mother saying I was trouble.

Anyway, Memorial weekend was approaching, and I couldn't find no one else to go with me to Myrtle Beach, S.C. I met this girl who was also leaving from New York. We rode the bus all the way down south together. I couldn't wait to get off that grey hound bus. It was very hot. Felt like 200 degrees on that bus.

While I was in MB, S.C. my friend from New York called me crying. I said, *"Hello, what is going on?"* She was on the other end of the phone. 800 miles away telling me her pimp boyfriend beat her up. I said, *"What? How do you know he was a pimp?"* She said, *"I was his main chick."* He had 13 girls working for him. I asked her, *"Do your mother think I was involved in this equation?"* The phone went dead. That's one thing there was never no reception on the cellular phones. I was about to hop on another bike. Anyway, she got beat up and I'm down south. Her mother was wrong about me!

2006

Voom, Voom, Voom

Memorial weekend Myrtle beach, S.C. back at it again. Bikers, pool parties, beach parties, barbecue, men, bikes, women, thick, fat, skinny, short, dark, light, medium complexion. Everybody was out from everywhere. Two o'clock in the morning riding to the racetrack with other bikers out. But not too many. My crew and I enjoyed being away from the New York streets, traffic, and noise.

Back when I took a trip to Virginia Beach, VA with my cousin. It was a nice walk along the boardwalk. We were able to rent bicycles. (You know I was used to motorcycles so riding a regular bike was as easy as one, two, three. My cousin is older than me and she struggled.) She said, *"Girl, I didn't ride one of these in years."* LOL.

Virginia Beach, the sand was filled with seashells, little rocks and a whole lot of people. Nowhere to put your beach blanket and relax. The sun was glistening and hot. Water was beautiful. Men, women and children wore bathing suits. No bar-b-ques or music. It was more family oriented than when I go to Myrtle Beach, S.C. for Memorial weekends.

Also in Ocean City, Maryland is a different kind of scene. There were bikes and hot guys but not too many. I didn't make that much money at the casino. I just broke even. The food was delicious. The night life was a little on the quiet side. But I enjoyed my trip to Ocean City.

BACK WHEN 2007

Voom, Voom, Voom

Miami Beach, FL. I was riding down the strip and guess who I saw. Dudes from New York. I'm like, *"Wow. What are you doing here?"* Leaving one state traveling to another state still running into familiar faces. Never know who you would run into. The way the saying goes *"You could run but you can't hide."* Miami Beach, flow, and weather already 83° at 10 a.m. everyone just coming outside at 4 p.m. in the afternoon to let the sun calm down. First stop was to get something to eat. Next stop was back in the room. *"What next?"* A little rest and then back outside.

Although, I loved riding and hanging out with my friends. There was more to me than just that. I was a boss, and a boss is a leader. Let's not make no mistakes a leader and never no follower. Back in 2004, I completed an all-natural hair course and now in 2007 I enrolled myself in Cosmetology School for the second time. I completed the course and one month before I graduated, I was looking for 10 models to allow me to demonstrate my skills. I found 15 models and after a few rehearsals some girls started dropping out.

Anyway, when it came to the day of the fashion show. I had 9 remaining models, a photographer and my DJ. The lounge it was held in was a small place on Guy R Brewer Blvd in Queens, New York. When I came out on stage, the DJ was bumping Neyo song Miss Independent, she got her own…

The crowd cheered, *"yes princess."*

The show was on a Saturday evening. When I came back to hair school on Monday for class, my instructor asked me in front of everybody, *"How was the fashion show?"* I said, *"Real nice."* The next week I bought the video of my fashion show to class. My instructor said, *"There are two types of people in this world. There's one type who talks and the second are doers. And Princess is a Doer."* The whole class was amazed. But back then they really didn't know who I was. A boss sitting in the class!

2008

Voom, Voom, Voom

This time all the bikers leaving from Springfield Blvd, and Linden Blvd., in Queens, New York. One guy I went to school with bought a motorcycle, took off his helmet. I'm sitting on my friend Stew bike.

Mark came to say, *"What's up?"*

I said *"Hey"*

He said, *"I didn't know you ride."*

I said, *"I just jump on the back."*

He said, *"Do you know how to braid?"*

I said, *"What?"*

He said, *"Do you still work in the salon?"*

I said, *"No"*

He said, *"Oh, I need my hair braided."*

I said, *"Thirty dollars."*

He said, *"Ok, when?"*

Stew came out the store and said, *"What's up to Mark."*

I said, *"Ya know each other?"*

He said, *"Yes, Stew is my man."*

I said, *"Do you know where he lives?"*

Stew said, *"We got to stop at my crib, I forgot something."*

Mark said, *"Ok, could you braid my hair now?"*

I said, *"Ok"*

In front of his house, sitting outside on the step. I braided Marks hair. In some simple corn braids. Now it's time for Mark to pay. *"I'll give you thirty-five."*

I said, *"Ok"*

Mark asked, *"Stew, do you have change for a hundred-dollar bill?"* Stew was checking his wallet. *"No, I'm sorry, all I have is seven dollars."*

I said, *"That's ok we could make change at the corner store."*

Mark said, *"I'll be right back."*

(Rode off on his bike to go to the store.) I waited a half hour. No Mark. Stew tried calling his cellular phone and it's going straight to his voicemail. I told Stew, *"When mark comes back, just give me a call."* I just wanted to go home to relax. *"I'll come back out and then we can finish riding."*

Two hours turned into three long hours. (No Mark) I was starting to wonder why would you approach me for your hair done and you not wanting to pay?

(God doesn't like ugly. Do unto people as you want done to you.) I called Stew the next day and told him what I didn't like about the whole situation. He said that it didn't have anything to do with him! It changed our friendship for a couple of weeks.

One hot, sunny day, I was going up Linden Blvd. ran into Bernard. One of Stew friends that we use to ride with last summer. Bernard said *"Hey, Princess."*

"What's going on?"

I said, *"Everything is good."*

He asked, *"How's Stew? Do you still ride?"*

I'm like, *"I ride with whoever I want to ride with at that time. But I'm not talking to your boy. We had an issue two weeks ago."* He said, *"That was your best friend, what happened?"* I told Bernard about his boy Mark not wanting to pay me for braiding his hair. And how *Stew, saying "It had nothing to do with him."* When everything took place in front of his house.

Chapter 7

Bernard called me one day. Ring, Ring, Ring.

I answered, he asked, *"Princess, are you busy?"*

I said, *"Just sitting here. I just finished eating some Jamaican food."*

"Do you want to go for a ride?"

I said, *"Sure, why not?"* we rode to Elmont Road where there were over 200 other bikers. It was no barbeque. Nothing planned. Just where all the bikes wanted to meet up. Music playing loud in the street. Guys doing stuns on their motorcycles. Women watched. Some with short shorts, see through tops, men wore wife beater t-shirts. (Loved the scenery, everyone enjoying themselves.) I hung out with Bernard all day long. He rode me home on his 1300 ninjas. It was ten in the evening. I then took a shower. My cellular was on my bed it started ringing. I ignored it to go to the bathroom. After I took a nice hot shower, I wanted to turn my phone off. I looked to see who called. I had a missed call from Bernard. I sure hope he didn't think I was coming back out to ride again. I called him back. Bernard picked up his phone. *"Princess, I got to tell you something."*

I asked, *"What happened?"*

He said, *"Do you know what happened to Mark?"*

I said, *"Mark who?"*

He said, *"The same mark that you braided his hair."*

I asked, *"what happened to him?"*

He said, *"He fell off of his bike on the Grand Central parkway and broke his foot."*

I said, *"Wow, how do you know that?"*

He said, *"Kenny and Dwayne were riding with him, and he hit a pot whole. They saw his bike go down and they pulled over to call the ambulance.*

I said, *"Wow, Bernard, I'm tired and I'll call you tomorrow."*

When I kneeled to pray. I said, *"Lord, I don't wish nothing bad on my enemies, heal every situation. Teach me to love my enemies. Father, have your way, Lord. Protect me and my family from danger. Amen."*

Mark played with a child of God. I belong to my heavenly father. No weapon formed against me will be able to prosper. I needed those thirty-five dollars when I braided his hair. And he took advantage. I couldn't tell Bernard on the phone but that's good for Mark!

Chapter 8

In April 2009, Danbury, Connecticut. We rode from New York a two-and-a-half-hour ride on the motorcycle. (What a long ride.) I was invited to attend a seafood feast with all the bikers from the East coast to the West coast. Women and Men bike clubs and auto clubs were all invited. One thing that I really loved was there was never no fights or quarrels among grown folks. The bikers were a little community all by itself.

Memorial Weekend, May

Voom, Voom, Voom

Back in the Myrtle Beach, S.C. different faces but you never get tired. One day this guy came up to me in the hotel lobby and asked me *"What are you doing here?"*

I said, *"Do I know you?"*

He said, *"No. but you come down here every year and you don't belong here."*

I was confused. I asked him, *"What do you mean?"*

He said. *"Ma, you are too pretty to be in Myrtle Beach, and you stand out from the crowd. You look way too good to be bike hopping. These girls that come down here are hoes."*

I said, *"Ok."* As I walked away into my feelings. He said, *"You should go home."* I rode with my friends that day but that night I was packing my clothes. I booked a one-way trip back to New York on spirit airlines. I pledged to myself, I'm not coming back to Myrtle Beach, S.C. for bike week no more!!

CHAPTER 9

In February 2013. It was a bad snowstorm, and everyone was outside trying to shovel the six-inch foot of snow from around their cars. Also, in front of their houses and up the steps leading to the front doors. I was in Copiague, long Island helping my boyfriend with the snow in front of his brother's house. I had on blue jeans, some gloves, a scarf, and my coat. The snow was so thick it was really cold, and I nearly frooze. I said, *"Williams, I'm going inside."* My nose was red, and my nose kept running. I started feeling sick. Williams, stayed outside for another two hours shoveling snow and he came in. He was such a sweetheart, made me a cup of tea. Then told me to drink soup. He said, with this weather all you need to do is drink something hot and rest.

That's what I did, went to bed and slept like a newborn baby. All I wanted to do was sleep. I would wrap myself up in a blanket and watch a little TV until I fell asleep. Monday mornings, I took the LIRR back to Jamaica, Queens where I lived. I went to work Monday to Thursday. Then spent time with Williams and his family from Friday through Monday morning. (Yes, that was my routine for eight months until one day I had a doctor's appointment.)

I was sitting in the waiting area after taking a urine test. The nurse came out to say *"Ms. Glover, come inside my office please."* I went in and Angela said, *"Sit down."*

I'm looking at her like *"What?"*

She said, *"Congratulations, you are positive."*

I said, *"What?"*

She said, *"yes, the pregnancy test shows you are 99.9% pregnant."*

I said, *"What?"* I couldn't believe it. Walking out the doctor's office not knowing who I'm going to tell first. My phone started ringing. Looking down to answer, it was my mother. I said, *"Hello."*

I got to the supermarket and there my mother was standing online at the register. I asked, *"Do you need help?"* She asked me, *"How was your doctor appointment? Did everything go well?"* Not giving me a chance to speak. She just kept talking and asking questions right there in the supermarket. I was quiet. She said, *"Here hold this bag."*

I turned and said, *"I'm pregnant."*

She said, *"What?"*

I said, *"that's what I said."*

She asked, *"Well, what are you going to do?"*

I said, *"I don't know."*

She asked, *"Did you tell Williams?"*

I said *"No"*

She said, *"well, what is he going to say?"*

I said, *"I don't know. I didn't tell him yet."*

She said, *"Is he going to be mad?"*

I'm like, *"I don't know."* For anybody that didn't know my mother. Well, that's how she was one question would turn into six to ten more. But you had to love her.

CHAPTER 10

November 8, 2014, Celebrating Sapphire's first birthday party. Wow, did she have a lot of guests. Everyone, I invited attended. I knew this little girl was going to be someone special. Christmas was about six weeks away, I felt she doesn't need another thing. People bought her so many toys, clothes, and books. We celebrated with family and friends, but one person didn't show up. Sapphire's older brother from her father's side. Everyone was asking for "C." I'm saying, *"Maybe he's running late."* His father calling his cellular phone not getting an answer. Anyway, you can expect teenagers to be into their friends and not wanting to hang around their family all the time.

As the day progressing party was going well, now it's time to cut the cake. Everyone sang, Happy Birthday…

Later that night, we arrived home. Not long after I put my baby girl to bed. Williams, wanted to talk in the living room. I told him how tired I was, and I needed to get some sleep. (It's been a long day.) he started the conversation saying, *"You noticed my son wasn't there for his sister's party."*

I said, *"Maybe he had other plans."*

He said, *"Well I asked him this morning was he planning on coming?"*

No comments. He started, this big argument about the boy being uncomfortable and all I care about is my family and friends.

I'm wondering to myself, well didn't your family come support the child's party also. Before you knew it. I got one blow in my arm. I was so tired, but I fought back. That negro lost his mind. Why are you putting your hands on me? Who cares if your son didn't come to a one-year-old birthday party? Who was there was supposed to be there! Now good night. Of course, Williams slept on the couch this night. (Along with many other nights.)

In the ending of December, I kept getting a pain in my side. Not much of an appetite, but my part time job at the day care gave a Christmas party with a lot of food. I took my plate to go. New Year's Day I took a pregnancy test. Results were positive.

2015

July 13, Sky Princess

This guardian angel was born. My precious darling, rolled out at 6:25 in the morning. She was a lot of work. Doctors said push and she kept going up and down my birth canal. I was pushing and doctors said, *"Make this one count."*

All I heard was a baby's cry.

That's why I dedicate this book to my two precious sunbeams.

CHAPTER 11

A boss isn't a man telling a woman what to do. A boss isn't a woman telling a man what to do. But a boss is someone who is in charge of handling business. *"Just because a woman drives the children to school every day, cook dinner, return emails, check messages, pick up toys and keep the house clean doesn't mean she's bossy!"*

CHAPTER 12

In my opinion, A women can be bossy because she has all these tasks. Any women who had contractions, bared labor pains, and delivered a child has every right to be bossy.

Back in the 1950's housewives stayed at home to raise the children and kept the house clean. *"Ok they were obedient."* Times changed now. Women want to drive nice luxurious cars too. Why? Because we could afford them too. A woman who has a child, it's her choice to stay home and raise that child or go out to work every day. She still can support her family after money's made to help pay the bills. There's car insurance, phone, cable, grocery money and mortgage. Let's not make no mistakes whether you are a man or a woman you learn discipline for those rainy days!

Now, women are CEOs of companies, principals, doctors, lawyers, teachers, judges, doing construction work, driving the bus and producing her own music.

Ladies, Boys and Girls be independent, and you will accomplish any goal or task life throws your way.

Stay tuned for part 2

"My journey to success"
followed by
"This is my version of being a Boss Lady."

R.I.P. Bernice Glover a.k.a. Mom the Real Boss.
Charlie pooh you will be missed
Aunty B, Ms. B, Butch and Les RIP

THE END........